Crochet Stars

Noreen Crone-Findlay

STACKPOLE
BOOKS

Essex, Connecticut
Blue Ridge Summit, Pennsylvania

With all my gratitude and love to the brightest shining stars in my constellation. To my beloveds: Jim, Chloe, Clancy, James, Angus, Alliston; to all our fur, feather, scale, and fin animal companions; and also to the deeply appreciated and cherished friends and family members who have been so loving and kind. And also with many, many huge thanks to my wonderful editor, Candi Derr, who makes magic happen.

Longtime friends are stars that sparkle in our constellation, and I am blessed to be long, longtime friends with Judy Wood and Sylvie Nicolas. Both of them are close to my heart and I treasure them so dearly, so this book is also dedicated to them. Bless their hearts!

STACKPOLE BOOKS

An imprint of Globe Pequot, the trade division of The Rowman & Littlefield Publishing Group, Inc.
4501 Forbes Blvd., Ste. 200
Lanham, MD 20706
www.rowman.com

Distributed by NATIONAL BOOK NETWORK
800-462-6420

British Library Cataloguing in Publication Information available

Library of Congress Cataloging-in-Publication Data
Names: Crone-Findlay, Noreen, author.
Title: Crochet stars : 25+ customizable projects full of love, laughter,
  and inspiration / Noreen Crone-Findlay.
Description: First edition. | Essex, Connecticut : Stackpole Books, [2024]
Identifiers: LCCN 2023048110 (print) | LCCN 2023048111 (ebook) | ISBN
  9780811774222 (paperback) | ISBN 9780811774239 (ebook)
Subjects: LCSH: Crocheting—Patterns. | Crocheting—Technique. | BISAC:
  CRAFTS & HOBBIES / Needlework / Crocheting | CRAFTS & HOBBIES /
  Folkcrafts
Classification: LCC TT825 .C783 2024 (print) | LCC TT825 (ebook) | DDC
  746.43/4041—dc23/eng/20231220
LC record available at https://lccn.loc.gov/2023048110
LC ebook record available at https://lccn.loc.gov/2023048111

♾™ The paper used in this publication meets the minimum requirements of American National Standard for Information Sciences—Permanence of Paper for Printed Library Materials, ANSI/NISO Z39.48-1992.

First Edition

Contents

Introduction

When my precious and beloved son-in-law died suddenly of a post-COVID heart catastrophe, I turned to my crochet hooks for respite. One of the most comforting and consoling things to make were Star Babies, based on a series of delightful dreams that I had enjoyed over the years. I talked with my wonderful editor, Candi Derr, about writing a book about crafting comfort to help move through the difficult path of grief and mourning. We focused on the crocheted stars, as they are such a powerful metaphor for finding our way through difficult times—humans have always used the stars to navigate. So this book evolved and has been a source of great consolation to me as our family walks the path of grief and mourns the loss of our darling Clancy and also as I adjust and learn to live with the difficulties of life with Long COVID. It's been a tough time, but yarn and crochet hooks are such a good way of moving forward, stitch by stitch, through the paradoxes of sorrows and celebrations. I hope that you will find delight in this little book—it is all about love—and may your life be full and rich and ripe with love too!

Hugs and blessings,
Noreen

Notes for Success

Abbreviations used in this book:

ch	chain
dc	double crochet
hdc	half double crochet
Rnd	Round
RS	right side of fabric
sc	single crochet
sl st	slip stitch
WS	wrong side of fabric

Finishing: Dampen the star and then place a pressing cloth over it to steam it lightly; or dampen the star and then pin the points to a foam or cork board and push into shape. Allow to dry. Weave in the yarn ends with a darning or tapestry needle. Trim any ends.

Finger wrap starting loop: Beginning at the center of the star, wrap the yarn around two fingers of your nondominant hand and pinch the tail of the yarn to your finger. Insert the hook under the wrap, yarn over, pull through to form the first part of a chain stitch on the hook. Yarn over again and pull through the loop. Slip the loop off your finger and now work Round 1 (the Center Round) into the loop, working over the loop and the tail. Pull up firmly to close the loop after the first round and join last sc to first sc.

My favorite way of joining one strand of yarn to another: Make a slipknot with the new strand of yarn. Take the end of the old strand of yarn through the slipknot. Slide the slipknot up to the place where you want the join to be, drop the old yarn end, and pull up snappily and hard on the tail of the new yarn and the yarn coming from the new ball. There will be a satisfying little pop as the yarn snaps the knot into place and firmly joins the new yarn.

When making a slipknot, either for joining a new strand of yarn or making the first loop of a starting chain or the wrapped finger loop, always work with the yarn that is coming from the ball and not the tail of yarn.

Decreasing over two stitches: Draw up a loop in the first stitch, then draw up a loop in the second stitch, yarn over, and pull through all loops on hook.

Pattern gauge: Exact gauge is not essential for these projects, but when you want the star to be firm, use a hook that is smaller than the one suggested on the label of the yarn. If you want a soft and drapey star, use a larger hook than recommended on the yarn label.

Changing the size of the finished project: To make a star larger, use a thicker yarn (or two strands of yarn held together) and a larger hook. To make it smaller, use thinner yarn and a smaller hook.

Making a surgeon's knot: Take end "A" over and under end "B" twice, then take end "B" over and under "A" once and pull up hard to lock the knot.

Working dc around the post of the dc in a previous round: Yarn over, insert the hook behind the vertical post of the dc in the previous round, taking the hook out in front of the next dc, yarn over, pull through, yarn over, pull through 2 loops on hook, yarn over, pull through the remaining 2 loops on the hook.

SMALL STARS

Glimmer Star

Have you heard about the power of "glimmers," the tiny, sweet things that lift you up, giving you a moment of respite, a shimmer of possibility? I think this usage originated from the phrase "glimmers of hope." Glimmers are essential in this frantic day and age, and so I dedicate this little Glimmer Star to all those moments of unexpected blessings and healing. May these stars bring you delight in the making of them! The finished size of the Glimmer Star depends on the size of crochet hook and thickness of yarn or thread.

SAMPLE STARS (PURPLE STARS)

* Yarn: Lion Brand Bonbons in #601-640 Nature; #2 fine weight; 100% cotton; 28 yd (26 m), 0.35 oz (10 g) per skein
* Hook: US size E-4 (3.5 mm) hook
* Finished size: 2½ in (6.5 cm) from tip to tip

See "Notes for Success" on page 5 for information about abbreviations, gauge, how to join yarns, how to decrease, how to change the size of the star, and how to finish the star.

INSTRUCTIONS

Note: To make two-color stars, work the center loop and Rnds 1 and 2 with first color. Cut yarn and join second color. Work points with second color.

Beginning at the center of the star, use the yarn wrap technique to make the starting loop (see page 5).

Rnd 1 (RS): Ch 1, 10 sc into yarn wrap loop. Join last sc to 1st sc.

Rnd 2: Ch 1, (1 sc in 1st sc, 2 sc in next sc, ch 2) 5 times. Join last ch to 1st sc. (15 sc)

Pull up hard on the tail to close the center.

Points:

*Row 1 (RS): Ch 1, 3 sc, turn.
Row 2: Ch 1, skip 1st sc, 1 sc in remaining 2 sc. Turn. (2 sc)
Row 3: Ch 1, skip 1st sc, 1 sc, do not turn. (1 sc)
Edge: Ch 1. Sl st in the edge of the last sc and then in the end stitches of the left-hand side edge of the point and into the ch-2 space.

Repeat from * 4 more times.

End by ch 1 and joining to the 1st sc of Row 1 of the 1st point. Cut yarn. Finish. Weave in ends.

For more options with the Glimmer Star, see Painted Stars on page 13, sample Eco-Friendly Stars on page 14, and Wire Stars on page 16.

Sweet Dreams Star

The Sweet Dreams Star is the last star that I designed for this book. It's the easiest and quickest star in the book and only takes a few moments to crochet, but it took me hundreds of iterations and experiments to come up with! I dreamed about this little star, jumped out of bed, wrote the pattern down, and then was tickled pink when it turned out to be exactly what I had hoped it would be. All those hundreds of stars that had to come and go before I could get to this final, delicious little star were all worth it! The finished size of the Sweet Dreams Star depends on the thickness of the yarn or thread and the size of the hook. Want a teeny tiny star? Use a small steel crochet hook and #10, #20, or #30 crochet cotton thread. Want a more substantial star? Use sport weight or bulky yarn, or T-shirt yarn and a size H-8 (5 mm) or larger hook. Super bulky yarn and a size K or L (8 mm) hook makes a cheerfully chunky star. Wire works well for the Sweet Dreams Star too (see page 16). The Sweet Dreams Star is a great choice for so many of the projects in this book: ornaments, quick and easy gifts, earrings, and more. Hope you have fun with it and, of course, may you have sweet dreams!

SAMPLE STARS

Yarn/Hook/Finished Size:
* Orange star, right: Lion Brand Bonbons (1 strand) in #601-610 Party; #3 light weight; 100% acrylic; 38 yd (35 m), 0.35 oz (10 g) per skein; and US size E-4 (3.5 mm) hook will make a star that is 1¾ in (4 cm) from point to point.
* White star, center: Lion Brand Bonbons (1 strand) in #601-640 Nature; #2 fine weight; 100% cotton; 28 yd (26 m), 0.35 oz (10 g) per skein; and US size E-4 (3.5 mm) hook will make a star that is 1¾ in (4 cm) from point to point.
* Small white star, top left: #10 crochet cotton (1 strand); #0 lace weight; and 0.75 mm hook will make a star that is 1 in (2.5 cm) from point to point.
* Painted star, bottom left: #10 crochet cotton (2 strands); #0 lace weight; and US size B-1 (2.25 mm) hook will make a star that is 1¾ in (4 cm) from point to point.
* Green star, left: T-shirt yarn, #2 sport weight, or #6 super bulky yarn and US size H-8 (5 mm) hook will make a star that is 3½ in (9 cm) from point to point.
* Blue and purple star, right: #7 jumbo yarn and a 7 mm (US K/L) hook will make a star that is 4 in (11 cm) from point to point.

* Copper star, center: 26 gauge wire and US size B-1 (2.25 mm) hook will make a star that is 2½ in (6 cm) from point to point.

> Please see "Notes for Success" on page 5 for information about abbreviations, gauge, how to join yarns, how to decrease, how to change the size of the star, and how to finish the star.

INSTRUCTIONS

Beginning at the center of the star, use the yarn wrap technique to make the starting loop (see page 5).

Rnd 1 (RS): Ch 1, 10 sc into starting loop. Join the last ch to the 1st sc with a sl st.

Rnd 2 (points): (Ch 5, sl st into 3rd ch from hook, ch 2, skip 1 sc, sl st into next sc) 5 times. End by joining to the 1st sl st of the ch 5 of the 1st point.

Cut yarn, leaving a tail the same length as the starting tail. Pull end through last loop on hook. Either weave in ends, taking them up to the tip of the 1st point and tying a knot to make a hanging loop, or tie a surgeon's knot (see page 5) on the back of the star and trim the ends close.

MEDIUM STARS

Gratitude Star

The Gratitude Star is a celebration and a reminder of all that makes our lives so precious. It's a thank-you with love in every stitch. It encompasses joy and sorrow, forgiveness and hope. It can light up the dark times and add zest to the delicious times.

SAMPLE STAR

* Yarn: Lion Brand Bonbons in #601-650 Party; #2 fine weight; 96% acrylic, 4% other fiber; 38 yd (35 m), 0.35 oz (10 g) per skein
* Hook: US size E-4 (3.5 mm) hook
* Finished size: 3½ in (9 cm) from point to point

> Please see "Notes for Success" on page 5 for information about abbreviations, gauge, how to join yarns, how to decrease, how to change the size of the star, and how to finish the star.

INSTRUCTIONS

Beginning at the center of the star, use the yarn wrap technique to make the starting loop (see page 5).

Rnd 1 (RS): Ch 1, 10 sc into loop. Join last sc to 1st sc in round.
Rnd 2: Ch 1, (1 sc in 1st sc, 2 sc in next sc) 5 times. Join last sc to 1st sc in round. (15 sc) Pull up very hard on the tail to close the opening at the center.
Rnd 3: Ch 1, 15 sc. Join last sc to 1st sc in round.
Rnd 4: Ch 1, 2 sc in each sc in round. Join last sc to 1st sc in round. (30 sc)
Rnd 5: (Ch 1, 6 sc, ch 2) 5 times, join to 1st sc of round.

Points:

The points are worked over the 6 sc groups that are separated by the ch-2 spaces.

*Row 1 (RS): Ch 2, 6 sc, turn.
Rows 2–6: Ch 1, skip 1st sc, 1 sc in each sc to end of row, turn. (You will have 5 sc after working Row 2 and 1 sc after Row 6.)
Edge: Ch 1, sl st in the end stitches of the left-hand side edge of the point down, ch 1 and sl st into the ch 2 space.

Repeat from * 4 more times.

End by ch 1 and joining to the 1st sc of Row 1. Cut yarn. Finish as described on page 5.

Clancy Star

I designed the Clancy star in honor of my darling son-in-law, who was the embodiment of loving kindness, quick wit, and great love of life and laughter, and the very dearest man. He was a star and is now among the stars and is held dear in our hearts. This star is all about love. Yes, love is eternal, isn't it?

SAMPLE STAR (LARGEST STAR)

* Yarn: Lion Brand Bonbons in #601-650 Party; #2 fine weight; 96% acrylic, 4% other fiber; 38 yd (35 m), 0.35 oz (10 g) per skein
* Hook: US size E-4 (3.5 mm) hook
* Finished size: 4½ in (11.5 cm) from point to point
Smaller stars were made with crochet cotton and smaller hooks.

> Please see "Notes for Success" on page 5 for information about abbreviations, gauge, how to join yarns, how to decrease, how to change the size of the star, and how to finish the star.

INSTRUCTIONS

Beginning at the center of the star, use the yarn wrap technique to make the starting loop (see page 5).

Rnd 1 (RS): Ch 4, (dc, ch 1) 14 times into loop. Join the last ch 1 in the 3rd ch of the starting ch. Pull up very hard on the tail to close the opening at the center.

Rnd 2: Ch 5, (dc around the post of each of the dc in the previous round [see page 5], ch 3) 14 times. Join the last ch 1 in the 3rd ch of the starting ch. Turn.

Points:

*Row 1 (RS): Ch 1, 3 sc in each of three of the next ch 3 spaces, turn.
Row 2: Ch 1, 9 sc, turn.
Rows 3–10: Ch 1, skip 1st sc, 1 sc in each sc to end of row, turn. (1 sc remains after Row 10.)
Edge: Ch 1, sl st in the end stitches of the left-hand side edge of the point down to the base of the point, ch 2.

Repeat from *4 more times.

End by joining to the 1st sc of Row 1. Cut yarn. Finish as described on page 5.

Flower Star

Combining flowers and stars may seem unlikely. But I was thinking about the phrase "the Earth laughs in flowers" and how many poets equate the stars with laughter. So it made sense to me that the laughter of the flowers and the stars should come together. And now they do.

SAMPLE STAR

* Yarn: Lion Brand Bonbons in #601-620 Pastels; #3 light weight; 100% acrylic; 28 yd (26 m), 0.35 oz (10 g) per skein
* Hook: US size C/D (3 mm) hook
* Gauge: 6 sc and 6 rows = 1 in (2.5 cm)
* Finished size: 4¾ in (12 cm) from point to point

Please see "Notes for Success" on page 5 for information about abbreviations, gauge, how to join yarns, how to decrease, how to change the size of the star, and how to finish the star.

INSTRUCTIONS

Beginning at the center of the star, use the yarn wrap technique to make the starting loop (see page 5).

Rnd 1 (RS): Ch 5, (1 hdc, ch 3) 4 times into the starting loop. Ch 3. Join with a sl st in the 2nd stitch of starting chain. Pull up on the tail end to close the starting loop.

Rnd 2: [(Ch 2, 1 sc, 1 hdc, 3 dc, 1 hdc, 1 sc) in ch-3 space] 5 times. Join with a sl st into the 1st ch-2 space of the round.

Rnd 3: (Ch 5, 1 sc in the ch-2 space between the petals of the previous round) 5 times.

Rnd 4: [(Ch 2, 1 sc, 3 hdc, 5 dc, 3 hdc, 1 sc) in ch-5 space] 5 times.

Rnd 5: (Ch 7, sc into the ch-2 space between the petals) 5 times.

Rnd 6: (Ch 3, 7 sc into ch-7 space) 5 times. Join last sc to 1st ch-3 space with a sl st.

Points:

The points are worked along each of the ch-7 spaces.

*Rows 1 and 2: Ch 1, 7 sc. Turn.
Rows 3–8: Ch 1, skip 1st stitch, 1 sc in each stitch to the end of the row. Turn.
Edge: Ch 1, sl st in the end stitches of the left-hand side edge of the point down and into the ch-3 space.

Repeat from * 4 more times.

End with 1 sc in the starting ch-3 space, ch 1, join to 1st sc of 1st point. Cut yarn. See Finishing notes on page 5.

Infinity and Beyond Star

When my husband, our kids, our grandson, and I say good-bye to each other, we always say, "Love you to infinity and beyond." That covers a lot of space, time, all that is, and more. The Infinity and Beyond Star is the largest star in this book and is the starting point of many of the projects.

SAMPLE STAR

* Yarn: Lion Brand Coboo Yarn in #157F Yellow; #3 light weight; 51% cotton, 49% rayon from bamboo; 232 yd (212 m), 3.5 oz (100 g) per skein
* Hook: US size G-6 (4 mm) crochet hook
* Finished size: 9 in (23 cm) from point to point

Please see "Notes for Success" on page 5 for information about abbreviations, gauge, how to join yarns, how to decrease, how to change the size of the star, and how to finish the star.

INSTRUCTIONS

Beginning at the center of the star, use the yarn wrap technique to make the starting loop (see page 5).

Rnd 1 (RS): Ch 1, 10 sc into yarn wrap loop. Pull up on the tail to close the opening at the center. Join last sc to 1st sc with a sl st.

Rnd 2: Ch 1, (1 sc in 1st sc, 2 sc in next sc) 5 times. Join last sc to 1st sc in round. (15 sc)

Rnd 3: 2 sc in each sc in round. Join last sc to 1st sc in round. (30 sc)

Rnds 4 and 5: Ch 1, 30 sc. Join last sc to 1st sc in round.

Rnd 6: Ch 1, 2 sc in each sc in round. Join last sc to 1st sc in round. (60 sc)

Rnd 7: Ch 1, (12 sc, ch 1) 5 times. Join last sc to 1st sc in round.

Rnd 8: (Ch 1, 12 sc, ch 2) 5 times. Join to 1st sc of round.

Points:

The points are worked over the 12 sc groups that are separated by the ch-2 spaces.

*Rows 1–11: Ch 1, skip 1st sc, 1 sc in each sc to end of row, turn. (You will have 11 sc after working Row 1 and 1 sc after working Row 11. Do not turn at the end of Row 11.)

Edge: Ch 1, sl st in the end stitches of the left-hand side edge of the point down into the ch-2 space.

Repeat from * 4 more times.

End by ch 1 and joining to the 1st sc of Row 1. Cut yarn. Follow Finishing instructions on page 5.

Spiral Nebula Star

Seeing amazing telescope images from space inspired me to design the Spiral Nebula Star. It celebrates the astonishing beauty of the vastness of our galaxy and the beauty of the spiral nebulas that cradle the stars.

SAMPLE STAR

* Yarn: Lion Brand Bonbons in #601-660 Celebrate; #2 fine weight; 96% acrylic, 4% other fiber; 38 yd (35 m), 0.35 oz (10 g) per skein
* Hook: US size B-1 (2.25 mm) hook
* Gauge: 7 sc and 7 rows= 1 in (2.5 cm)
* Finished size: 6.5 in (16.5 cm) from point to point

> Please see "Notes for Success" on page 5 for information about abbreviations, gauge, how to join yarns, how to decrease, how to change the size of the star, and how to finish the star.

INSTRUCTIONS

Note: All stitches other than in round 1 are worked only into the back bar of the previous round.

Beginning at the center of the star, use the yarn wrap technique to make the starting loop (see page 5).

Rnd 1 (RS): Ch 5, (1 hdc, ch 3) 4 times into the starting wrapped loop. Ch 3. Join with a sl st in the 2nd ch of starting chain.

Rnd 2: Ch 2, (3 hdc, ch 5) in each ch-3 space. Join last ch to 2nd ch of starting ch.

Rnds 3 and 4: Ch 2, (1 hdc in each hdc in cluster, 1 hdc in the 1st ch in the ch-5 space, ch 5) 5 times. Join last ch to 2nd ch of starting ch. (There are 4 hdc in each cluster in Rnd 3, 5 hdc in each cluster in Rnd 4.)

Rnds 5 and 6: Ch 2, (1 hdc in each hdc in cluster, 1 hdc in the 1st 2 ch of the ch-5 space, ch 5) 5 times. Join last ch to 2nd ch of starting ch. (There are 7 hdc in each cluster in Rnd 5, 9 hdc in each cluster in Rnd 6.)

Points:

*Row 1 (RS): 1 sc in the back bar of each of 9 hdc, 1 sc in the back bar of the 1st 2 ch of the ch-5 space, turn. (11 sc)

Row 2: Ch 1, 11 sc in the back bar of the sc in the previous row, turn.

Rows 3, 5, 7, 9, and 11 (RS): Ch 1, skip 1st sc, 1 sc in the back bar of each of the sc in the previous row, turn.

Rows 4, 6, 8, and 10 (WS): Ch 1, 1 sc in the back bar of each of the sc in the previous row to the last 2 sc of the row, work a decrease over the last 2 sc (see page 5), turn.

Row 12: Ch 1, skip 1 sc, 1 sc, turn.

Tip of Point: Ch 1, sl st in the edge of the last sc.

Edge: Work 1 sl st in each end stitch of the left-hand side edge of the point down to Rnd 6 of the center, ch 5.

Repeat from * 4 more times.

End by joining to the 1st sc of Row 1. Cut yarn. Finish as instructed on page 5. Weave in ends.

PROJECTS

Painted Stars

The Painted Stars can be used in so many fun ways! They are great as little gifts or holiday ornaments. They can be used to make jewelry or to embellish note cards, book covers, garlands, mobiles, frames, and more.

It's best to use light colored, 100% cotton to crochet the stars and then paint them with acrylic paints in any combination of colors that you like. This opens up all kinds of creative possibilities!

SAMPLE STARS

Yarn: The smallest stars are crocheted with #10 crochet cotton. The larger ones are crocheted with Lion Brand Bonbons in #601-640 Nature; #2 fine weight; 100% cotton; 28 yd (26 m), 0.35 oz (10 g) per skein.

INSTRUCTIONS

1. Crochet stars using the Glimmer, Gratitude, and Sweet Dreams patterns. It's a good idea to crochet a few extra of the Sweet Dreams star on page 7 to experiment with and to get a sense of how the paint will behave on the yarn. Leave yarn tails to make hanging loops. Weave the tails over to the tip of one point and then tie a knot at the end and trim. If you don't want hanging loops, tie a surgeon's knot (see page 5) at the back of the star and trim the ends.

2. Dampen the star and paint with diluted acrylic paints. You can add more color after the paint dries if the star needs touching up. Paint both sides of the star if it's going to be seen from both sides.

The stars in the photo have a dab of yellow at the center, one or two shades of blue next, and then iridescent purple at the tips.

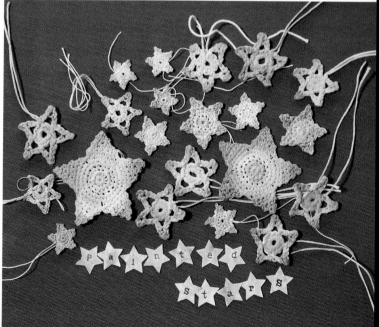

I love experimenting to see if, with a little imagination, something that might not normally be used as yarn can be rescued and reclaimed for a new use. The photo shows the Glimmer Star crocheted with some fun "rescues."

SAMPLE STARS

Yarn/Hook/Finished Size:
* Surveyor's tape (1) crocheted with a US size K-10½ (6.5 mm) hook makes a star that is 5 in (12.5 cm) from tip to tip.
* T-shirt yarn (2) crocheted with a US size H-8 (5 mm) hook makes a star that is 4½ in (11.5 cm) from tip to tip.
* Crochet thread (3) purchased from thrift shops, estate sales, and garage sales, crocheted with a US size 16 (0.6 mm) hook makes a star that is ¾ in (2 cm) from tip to tip. Crocheted with a US size 14 (0.75 mm) hook, it makes a star that is 1 in (2.5 cm) from tip to tip.

* Cloth tea bags cut into fabric strips (4) and crocheted with a US size H-8 (5 mm) hook make a star that is 4 in (10 cm) from tip to tip. See https://youtu.be/WOaSszWntrU for how to make the yarn.
* Cloth strip yarn from a worn-out shirt (5) crocheted with a US size H-8 (5 mm) hook makes a star that is 4 in (10 cm) from tip to tip.
* 30 gauge wire (6) crocheted with a US size 7 (1.5 mm) hook makes a star that is 1¼ in (3.5 cm) from tip to tip.

More upcycled projects:
* *Upcycled Tote Bag, page 15*
* *Memory Star made with upcycled T-shirt yarn, page 19*
* *Mending, page 16*

Upcycled tote Bag

This thrift shop tote bag was brand new and made of really nice recycled cotton (the label said) but had a big logo printed on it. I had no idea what the logo was advertising. I happily covered it up with a slew of crocheted stars using the patterns I designed for this book. I embellished it with thrift shop beads. This is a great way to upcycle all kinds of garments and accessories. Got a T-shirt, hat, or jacket with an unwanted logo? Crochet stars to the rescue!

I pinned the stars on and stitched them in place by hand. If you prefer, you can sew the stars on by machine. Many of the stars on the bag were "tests" of early versions of the patterns. I used crochet cotton from thrift shops to double up the upcycled goodness.

More upcycled projects:
* *Eco-Friendly Stars: Upcycled and Rescued "Yarns," page 14*
* *Memory Star made with upcycled T-shirt yarn, page 19*
* *Mending, page 16*

Mending

When my favorite shirt got mysterious stains—bike chain? something in the gardening shed?—that refused to go away in the wash, it struck me that covering up the offending stains with stars was the perfect solution, so I crocheted a Gratitude Star and two Glimmer Stars and stitched them to the shirt. Then, when my favorite black and white T-shirt popped a hole, I thought, *Aha! Stars to the rescue!* I crocheted a Flower Star with #10 crochet cotton to cover the mending stitches and embellished a tee that I didn't want to toss. Years ago, my daughter gave me a cozy shawl that I love and use almost every day. It has started to get little holes, so I now crochet Glimmer and Sweet Dreams Stars to embellish and repair the much-loved shawl.

Wire Stars

Crocheting wire is very hard on your hands, tendons, joints, and shoulders, so if you have issues with or pain in your wrists, hands, arms, shoulders, or neck, do not work with wire. That being said, wire is very pretty when crocheted. It's important to go slowly and not hold tightly to the wire. The thinner the wire, the better it is for crochet. Beading wire that is 30 gauge or finer is best. Even though wire is cranky to work with, I couldn't resist including wire crochet in this book because sparkly stars in such a durable and flexible medium are so inviting!

SAMPLE STARS (in photo, left to right)

Yarn/Hook/Finished Size:
* Gratitude Star (see page 8) crocheted with 30 gauge wire and a US size B-1 (2.25 mm) hook. The Gratitude Star is 3½ in (9 cm) from point to point.

* Glimmer Star (see page 6) crocheted with 30 gauge wire and a US size 7 (1.5 mm) hook. The Glimmer Star is 1¼ in (3 cm) from point to point.
* The Sweet Dreams Star is definitely the easiest star pattern for wire (see page 7); this one was crocheted with 26 gauge wire and a US size B-1 (2.25 mm) hook. The Sweet Dreams Star is 2 in (5 cm) from point to point.

Smiling Star Stuffy, Pin, Fob, or Ornament

Many years ago, I had the most delightful dream. In the dream, the Northern Lights were flashing through the sky, and there was a wonderful sound of musical laughter. Suddenly, a cascade of tumbling, chuckling, chortling, and uproariously laughing little stars came zooming down the Aurora Borealis as if it were a slide. It was completely enchanting! I have made many different versions of the laughing stars over the years and, of course, I had to design some for this book! The Smiling Stars can be made in different sizes, depending on the size of hook and thickness of yarn that you choose.

Smiling Stars use the Gratitude Star pattern (see page 8). The finished size depends on whether you use one strand of yarn and a smaller hook or two strands held together with a hook that is one or more sizes larger. So many options! It's a perfect pocket "fidget" toy or comfort stuffy and also makes a great hanging ornament or fob for your favorite pouch, pair of scissors, or key chain if you don't stuff it.

Note: Do not give babies, small children, or pets a stuffy that has beads sewn on—that is a choking hazard. Instead, make the eyes with embroidery floss or yarn.

SAMPLE STARS

* Yarn: Lion Brand Coboo Yarn in #157F Yellow; #3 light weight; 51% cotton, 49% rayon from bamboo; 232 yd (212 m), 3.5 oz (100 g) per skein.
* Hook: The larger star was crocheted with 2 strands of yarn held together using a US size G-6 (4 mm) hook. The smaller star was crocheted with a single strand of yarn and a US size B-1 (2.25 mm) hook.
* Gauge: Larger star—4 sc and 5 rows = 1 in (2.5 cm) with 2 strands of yarn held together. Smaller star—6 sc and 7 rows = 1 in (2.5 cm) with 1 strand of yarn.
* Finished sizes: Larger star—5 in (12.5 cm) from point to point. Smaller star—3 in (7.5 cm) from point to point.

Also needed: Stuffing, 2 black beads (6 mm in diameter for the larger star and 6/0 beads for the smaller star), a needle and thread to sew the beads on, black embroidery floss, tapestry or darning needle, light orange or pink pencil crayon for cheeks, scissors, light weight ⅝ in wide (1.5 cm wide) and 8 in long (20 cm long) ribbon for hanging if the Smiling Star is

going to be used as an ornament, and a jump ring and lobster claw closure for the fob.

INSTRUCTIONS

With yellow yarn and 2 strands of yarn and a US size G-6 (4 mm) hook for larger star or 1 strand of yarn and size B-1 (2.25 mm) hook for smaller star, crochet 2 stars (one for the front and one for the back) using the Gratitude Star pattern (page 8).

* Eyes: Sew 2 beads to the face on Rnd 3. Secure the ends on the back side of the face.
* Mouth: Embroider the smile in the ditch between Rnds 2 and 3, anchoring the embroidery floss on the wrong side of the face. Take the thread through to the front, over one stitch, and then to the back again. Come up through the face one stitch over and back through to the back. Repeat for the length of the smile.
* Cheeks: Rub colored pencil, crayon, or blush onto the cheeks.

Note: If the center of the face is too open, stitch into the center round on the back side of the face and pull up hard to pull the center completely closed. Stitch in place on the back of the face to secure the stitching.

Assembly:

Sew the back of the head to the front, leaving an opening for stuffing if you are making the stuffy.

Insert stuffing and sew the opening closed.

Do not leave an opening or stuff the Smiling Star if you are making the fob.

Take all ends inside.

* Hanging ribbon for the ornament: Thread one end of the ribbon into a craft or darning needle and take it through the top point of the star. Pull up and tie a knot in the ends.
* Fob: Use a pair of needle-nose pliers to open the jump ring and slip it into a loop on the tip of the top point. Slip the ring of the lobster claw clasp onto the jump ring and close the ring with the pliers.

Scrubby Stars

The Scrubby Stars in the photo were made using the Infinity and Beyond Star (page 11), Clancy Star (page 9), and Flower Star (page 10) patterns, but they can be made with any combination of the star patterns in this book. They are simple to make: just crochet a star using a "scrubby" yarn, and if you would like, work a round of sc around the outside edge. The stars in the photo were made with special yarn from Lion Brand, but if you can't find it, my clever editor, Candi Derr, substitutes tulle fabric netting cut into strips.

SAMPLE STARS

* Yarn: Lion Brand Stitch Soak Scrub Yarn in #781-106AA Turquoise; #4 medium weight; 100% nylon; 92 yd (84 m), 1.4 oz (40 g) per skein. Each ball makes four or more Scrubbies, depending on which pattern you choose.
* Hook size: US size H-8 (5 mm) hook.
* Finished sizes: Infinity Star—8 in (20 cm) point to point. Flower Star—6½ in (16.25 cm) point to point. Clancy Star—5 in (12.5 cm) point to point.

INSTRUCTIONS

Crochet a star with scrubby yarn or tulle using the Infinity and Beyond Star (page 11), Clancy Star (page 9), or Flower Star (page 10) patterns (or your choice of star patterns). Weave in the ends. *Do not press.*

The Gratitude and Clancy Stars are good choices to make brooches or shawl pins when crocheted with thin yarns or threads. Stitch on smaller crocheted stars, beads, buttons, charms, and found objects to embellish the front.

See steps 1, 2, and 3 of the Mobile Star on page 21 for instructions on how to make a stabilized star using mat board. An alternative option of assembling the "star sandwich" is to sew them together instead of working a single crochet edging. Optional: Paint the mat board star with acrylic paint before assembling the star sandwich.

Sew a pin to the back and enjoy!

Memory Star

The Memory Star is crocheted with T-shirt yarn made by cutting up a T-shirt that has either been outgrown or once belonged to someone whom you loved who has died. The center is a photo that has either been scanned or printed directly onto photo paper. A circle of cardboard supports the photo, and a circle of plastic protects it. You can slip little notes in between the layers, too, if you would like. A circle of fabric cut from the T-shirt is gathered to make a large "yo-yo circle," which holds all the layers together. The photo section is glued or stitched to a star crocheted with T-shirt yarn using the Clancy Star pattern on page 9, if you would like a larger star, or the Gratitude Star on page 8, if you prefer a slightly smaller star. This is a great way of reusing a favorite T-shirt and keeping loving memories alive.

SAMPLE STAR

* Yarn: Cut up a T-shirt into yarn (cut the strips about ½ in [1 cm] wide and wind into a ball. If you don't know how to make T-shirt yarn, check YouTube, as there are lots of how-to videos that will show you). *Note: One adult size T-shirt is enough. If you are using children's sizes, you may need more than one T-shirt. T-shirt yarn is equivalent to #5 bulky weight.*
* Hook: US size K-10½ (6.5 mm) hook
* Finished size: 11 in (28 cm) from point to point

Also needed: A photo of the person being celebrated, a 4 in (10 cm) square of cardboard, a 4 in (10 cm) square of plastic (the top from a salad container or a page protector both work), scissors, craft glue or a hot glue gun, needle and thread, optional dowel (if the side points of the star droop, a dowel will support them).

> Please see "Notes for Success" on page 5 for information about abbreviations, gauge, how to join yarns, how to decrease, how to change the size of the star, and how to finish the star.

INSTRUCTIONS

1. Make the T-shirt yarn and roll it into a ball. Set aside the sleeves and the upper part of the T-shirt above the sleeves.

2. Crochet the Clancy Star on page 9. Dampen it and flatten it out, finger pressing it into place. Allow it to dry completely before attaching the photo section to it.

3. Cut out 4 in (10 cm) diameter circles from the photo, a piece of cardboard, a circle of plastic, and if you are including a note, a piece of blank paper.

4. Cut a circle of the T-shirt fabric that is 5½ in (14 cm) in diameter. Fold the edge over approximately ⅛ in (0.25 cm) and gather it by stitching by hand slightly in from the folded edge.

5. Stack the cardboard circle, note (if writing one), photo, and plastic circle, and place them into the fabric "yo-yo" circle. Pull up on the thread to gather and secure the stitching. Stitch in place several times to secure the stitching. Stitch around the edge one more time and secure by stitching in place.

6. Edging: Work ch st for about 16 in (40 cm). Glue the chain-stitch trim around the edge of the photo. If needed, add a second round of chain-stitch cord around the outside of the photo section.

7. Glue or stitch the photo piece to the wrong side of the Clancy Star so the raised circle is outward.

8. Stitch a hanging ring to the top point, or frame the Memory Star.

9. If the side points droop, cut a dowel or sturdy wire the length of the span between the point tips, and paint it to match the T-shirt yarn. Stitch in place.

More upcycled projects:
* *Upcycled Tote Bag, see page 15*
* *Eco Friendly Stars: Upcycled and Rescued "Yarns," see page 14*
* *Mending, see page 16*

This is more of a recipe than a pattern—it's all about being playful. Experiment with combining your favorite beads with the small-, medium-, and large-size crocheted stars in whatever yarns speak to you. The star-shaped beads are wooden and were unfinished when I searched online and found them. I painted them in my favorite colors. The Star Mobile needs to live inside the house, because the large and medium stars have mat board liners for stability and wouldn't be able to survive rain or snow.

SAMPLE STARS

* Yarn: The Glimmer (page 6) and Gratitude Stars (page 8) were crocheted with Lion Brand Bonbons in #601-650 Party and #601-660 Celebrate; #2 fine weight; 100% cotton; 28 yd (26 m), 0.35 oz (10 g) per skein. I designed the mobile before I designed the Sweet Dreams star, so there aren't any in the pictured mobile, but I highly recommend adding some. The large foundation star is the Infinity Star (page 11) crocheted with Lion Brand 24/7 Cotton Yarn in #098C Ecru; #4 worsted weight; 100% mercerized cotton; 186 yd (170 m), 3.5 oz (100 g) per skein.
* Hooks: Large Infinity Star and medium stars—US size G-6 (4 mm) hook. Small stars—US size B-1 (2.25 mm) hook.
* Finished sizes: Large Infinity Star—8 in (20 cm) from point to point. Medium stars—4 in (10 cm) from point to point. Small stars—1½ to 2 in (4 to 5 cm) from point to point.

Also needed: Glass beads (2/0 size), needle and thread that fit through the beads, wooden star-shaped beads (¾ in/2 cm from point to point), paint, mat board to make stabilizing liners for the Infinity and Gratitude Stars, sharp craft knife to cut the liner stars out, pencil, and a cutting surface to cut the liner stars out.

> Please see "Notes for Success" on page 5 for information about abbreviations, gauge, how to join yarns, how to decrease, how to change the size of the stars, and how to finish the stars.

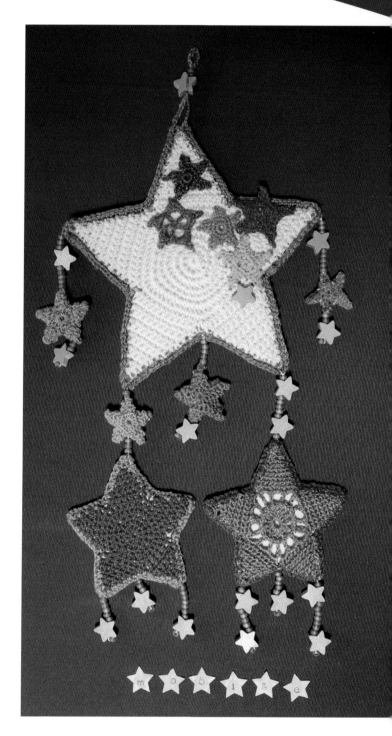

INSTRUCTIONS

Crochet the stars:

1. Large foundation star: Crochet 2 stars (1 for the front and 1 for the back) following the instructions for the Infinity Star on page 11.

2. Trace the large star onto mat board. Draw a line inside the first outline about ⅛ in (0.25 cm) away from the first line. Cut out the star, following the inside line, with a sharp craft knife.

3. Edging: Hold the front of the large star to the back of the large star, capturing the mat star inside the crocheted layers in a "star sandwich." With contrasting yarn, work sc through both layers of the crocheted stars to lock the 3 layers together. The edging of the large star in the photo was crocheted with blue yarn and then a round of sc in gold yarn.

4. Medium-size stars: Crochet 2 stars in each color (1 for the front and 1 for the back) following the instructions for the Gratitude Star on page 8 (4 medium-size stars in total).

5. Make 2 medium stars with mat board, following the instructions in step 2.

6. Crochet the fronts to the backs of the medium stars, following the instructions in step 3.

7. Small applique stars: Crochet 5 stars using the Sweet Dreams Star (page 7) and Glimmer Star (page 6) patterns. Sew them to the large star. Weave in any ends.

8. Hanging small stars: Crochet a front and back for each of the small stars using the Sweet Dreams Star (page 7) and Glimmer Star (page 6) patterns. The mobile in the photo has 4 hanging small stars, so 8 small stars were crocheted in total. Cut the yarn end, leaving an 8 in (20 cm) tail for stitching. The small stars do not need mat board liners. Stitch one back to each front using one of the yarn tails. Leave the remaining yarn tails for the assembly.

Assembly:

9. Lay the crocheted stars out on a flat surface in a configuration that appeals to you.

10. Hanging loop: Join yarn to the top point of the large star and ch 10. *Take the hook out of the last chain. Pull up the loop to lengthen it and thread it through a darning or tapestry needle. Take the needle and loop through the hole in the star shape bead; then remove the needle and place the loop back on the crochet hook.* Ch 20. Repeat from * to *. Ch 10. Rejoin yarn to the tip of the point. Stitch in place to secure. Cut yarn, thread end into darning needle and weave ends into the edge of the star. Trim the ends.

11. Side-hanging small stars and small star at lower edge of the large star: Using the yarn tails from the small stars, stitch 1 bead and 1 star bead and then 2 or 3 beads to one point, take the yarn through the star, pick up more beads and another star bead, then a couple of glass beads, and stitch to the side point. Stitch in place several times to secure. Take the yarn back down through the beads and into the small star, stitching in place several times again to secure the beads and stars. Weave the ends inside the stars.

12. Attaching the medium-size stars: Use the yarn color of the star to attach the embellishment beads. Start by joining the yarn to upper point of the medium-size star, burying the ends inside the star and then stitching in place to secure the yarn. Take the needle through the embellishment beads (do this with the small star on the left-hand medium star as well). Pick up the glass and wooden beads. Go back up through the column of beads and into the tip of the large star. Stitch in place to secure. Go back down through the beads to the medium star and stitch in place to secure. Weave in the ends.

13. Beads at lower edge of medium stars: Join a 24-in (60-cm) length of yarn, securing it by stitching in place. Pick up the glass beads, a star bead, if desired, and then a single glass bead. Take the needle back up through the column of beads and stitch in place in the medium star. Weave the needle over to the middle of the star for the next column of beads and repeat. Repeat again at the second point on the lower edge of the star. See the photo for placement.

The Star Garland can be made with any combination of the stars in this book. The garland in the photo was made by pinning the stars together with small brass safety pins that had seed beads slipped onto the pin before closing. This allows the garland to be reconfigured according to whim or need. Make the garland as long as you want using the pinning technique or, if you prefer, sew the stars together, joining two points and adding beads between them.

SAMPLE STARS

Yarns: Any yarn that you like. Crochet the stars using hooks that are at least one size smaller than recommended on the yarn label to give a firm finish to the star.

Also needed: Small brass safety pins, seed beads.

INSTRUCTIONS

Crochet as many stars as you like using any of the patterns in this book. Insert a pin into one point of a crocheted star, and then slip some beads onto the pin. Add the next star and close the pin. Voilà! The garland grows!

Spiral Nebula Star Trivet

The Spiral Nebula Star Trivet is equally at home under a tea-pot, plant pot, special flower from the garden, or perhaps just whirling at the center of your table. Crochet it with cream or white yarn for a winter holiday place setting.

SAMPLE STAR

* Yarn: Lion Brand Coboo Yarn (2 strands held together) in #109T Steel Blue; #3 light weight; 51% cotton, 49% rayon from bamboo; 232 yd (212 m), 3.5 oz (100 g) per skein
* Hook: US size G-6 (4 mm) hook
* Finished size: 11 in (28 cm) from point to point

Gratitude Star Coasters

Gratitude Stars are quick and easy to crochet for coasters, and they make great gifts. Use two strands of yarn held together for a firm and sturdy table accessory.

SAMPLE STAR

* Yarn: Lion Brand Coboo Yarn (2 strands held together) in #109T Steel Blue; #3 light weight; 51% cotton, 49% rayon from bamboo; 232 yd (212 m), 3.5 oz (100 g) per skein
* Hook: US size G-6 (4 mm) hook
* Finished size: 6 in (15 cm) from point to point

A magic wand is an innocent way of imagining and wishing for good things. So here are some Magic Wands to help bring all kinds of sweetness and goodness into the world!

SAMPLE STARS

* Yarn: Large (Gratitude) and small (Glimmer) stars—2 skeins of Lion Brand Bonbons in #601-660 Celebrate; #2 fine weight; 96% acrylic, 4% other fiber; 38 yd (35 m), 0.35 oz (10 g) per skein; Painted (Gratitude) Star—#10 crochet cotton (2 strands held together).
* Hooks: Large and small stars—US size G-6 (4 mm) hook; Painted Star—US size B-1 (2.25 mm) hook.
* Gauge: Large and small stars—5 sc and 5 rows = 1 in (2.5 cm) with two strands of yarn held together; Painted Star: 8 sc and 8 rows = 1 in (2.5 cm).
* Finished sizes: Small Magic Wand—1⅝ in (5.5 cm) from point to point, 5½ in (14 cm) tall; Large Magic Wand—4¼ in (11 cm) from point to point, 10 in (25 cm) tall; Painted Star Magic Wand: 3 in (7.5 cm) from point to point, 7½ in (19 cm) tall.

Also needed: Stick for handle (bamboo chopstick, 9 in/24 cm long for larger wand; 5 in/12.5 cm long bamboo lollipop stick for smaller wand, or cut ¼ in/0.5 cm dowel to desired length); the Painted Star Magic Wand uses an upcycled thrift store find of a painted wooden pen (with the empty pen cartridge removed); craft glue; ribbons; gold paint; beads, buttons, or charms and needle and thread to sew them on; a small amount of stuffing.

> Please see "Notes for Success" on page 5 for information about abbreviations, gauge, how to join yarns, how to decrease, how to change the size of the stars, and how to finish the stars.

INSTRUCTIONS

1. Crochet the star: With 2 strands of yarn held together and a US size G-6 (4 mm) hook, crochet 2 stars for each Magic Wand (you need a front and a back star) using the

Gratitude pattern for the larger star and the Glimmer pattern for the smaller Magic Wand. The Painted Star is crocheted with 2 strands of #10 crochet cotton held together, using a US size B-1 (2.25 mm) hook and the Gratitude Star pattern.

2. Paint the chopstick or lollipop stick gold.

3. Embellish the star with beads, buttons, or charms.

4. Glue the top of the stick to the inside of one of the stars.

5. Stitch the edges of the front of the star to the back of the star, leaving an opening for stuffing.

6. Stuff the larger star and sew the opening closed. The smaller stars don't need stuffing.

7. Tie a ribbon or chain stitch cord to the wand and then stitch it to the star. Embellish the ends with beads. Finish as on page 5.

Little Gifts

I never leave home without a little tin or pouch of "comfort gifts" in my pocket. People who follow my blog or social media will be familiar with my Comfort Bears. I also like to tat tiny butterflies and now, after designing the projects and writing this book, I carry little crocheted stars in my pocket. You never know when you are going to have a chat with someone who is going through something difficult and needs a little comfort or who is celebrating a special happening. It means so much to people to receive a little bit of unexpected kindness. It's lovely for you and for them! The Sweet Dreams Stars and Glimmer Stars are quick and easy to crochet, so you can make a lot of them with odds and ends of your stash. And they are such small projects that you can keep a pouch in your bag with the makings of them, to have them close at hand for on-the-go crocheting. Having a tin or little bag to hold the finished ones in your pocket, just ready for spreading a little comfort and joy, is simply delightful! It's also fun to leave stars hanging in libraries, restaurants, or other places to give a little happiness anonymously. I suggest that you make hang tags that say things like "You get a gold star," "I made this for you," or "Here's a little star to wish upon."

See the Embellished Note Card on page 30 if you'd like to mail some little stars to friends.

Embellished Sketchbook, Notebook, or Journal

A plain sketchbook, notebook, or journal can be embellished with your choice of the crocheted stars. The sketchbook in the photo was slathered with Mod Podge, and then the stars were squished in and also covered with the Mod Podge. Painted Stars (page 13) are especially pretty for embellishing book covers.

Picture Frame

This star frame is a lovely way to celebrate someone special. The frame in the photo was embellished with painted Glimmer Stars, but feel free to embellish with buttons, beads, charms, and found objects.

SAMPLE STAR

* Yarn: Lion Brand Yarn Bonbons in #601-640C Nature; #2 fine weight; 100% cotton; 28 yd (26 m), 0.35 oz (10 g) per skein
* Hook: US size E-4 (3.5 mm) hook
* Gauge: 6 sc and 6 rows = 1 in (2.5 cm)
* Finished size: 7 in (18 cm) from point to point

Also needed: A copy of a favorite photo, plastic from salad container to protect the photo, mat board to make stabilizing liners for the star, sharp craft knife, pencil, a cutting surface to cut the liner stars out, scissors, and pins or small clips or clamps to hold the layers of the star together during assembly.

Please see "Notes for Success" on page 5 for information about abbreviations, gauge, how to join yarns, how to decrease, how to change the size of the star, and how to finish the star.

INSTRUCTIONS

1. Back of frame: crochet the Infinity and Beyond Star following the instructions on page 11.

2. Trace the star onto mat board. Draw a line inside the first outline about ⅛ in (0.25 cm) away from the outside line. Cut out the star, following the inside line, with a sharp craft knife.

3. Trace the cardboard star onto the plastic and cut it out. Lay the plastic star on top of the photo (or scanned photo) and decide how you want the photo to be centered in the frame. Trace around the star and cut out the photo.

4. Front of frame:

Points:

*Ch 13.

Row 1 (RS): 1 sc in 2nd ch from hook and in each remaining ch. Turn. (12 sc)

Rows 2–11: Ch 1, skip 1st sc, 1 sc in each sc to end of row, turn. (1 sc will remain after working Row 11. Do not turn at the end of Row 11.)

Edge: Ch 1, sl st in the end stitches of the left-hand side edge of the point down to the last sc of Row 1*.

Repeat from * 4 more times.

Center Rounds:

Rnd 1 (RS): Ch 1, work 12 sc across the 1st row of each of the 5 points. Join the last sc to the 1st. (60 sc)

Rnd 2: Ch 1, 60 sc, join last sc to 1st.

Rnd 3: Ch 1, 1 sl st in each sc. Join last sl st to 1st. Cut yarn. Pull end through last loop on hook.

Assembly:

5. Lay the mat board star on the star back, then the photo, and then the plastic. Place the front on top and either pin the front crocheted star to the back or use small clamps to hold all the layers together.

6. Edging: Work around the outside of the star frame, working sc through both layers of the crocheted stars, capturing and locking the 5 layers together. At the top point, ch 30 to make a hanging loop. Join the last sc to the first and make sure that all ends are inside the star.

7. Embellish with small crocheted stars or buttons, beads, charms, or found objects.

Earrings

The Sweet Dreams Stars and Glimmer Stars can be made in several different ways for unique earrings. See the Wire Stars on page 16 and Painted Stars on page 13. The stars don't have to match each other exactly. Feel free to experiment with different combinations of beads for embellishment.

As well as your crocheted stars, you'll need needle-nose pliers, a package of earring findings, and a selection of beads. Attach a wire to the top point of the star, slide on some beads, twist a loop, and take it through the little ring of the earring. Voilà! Quick and easy earrings!

Note Cards

To make personalized cards, glue the Glimmer and Sweet Dreams Stars to the front of a premade blank card, or fold a piece of card stock to make a card. Write a message on the front and inside, and maybe add a couple of little stars with hanging loops to make a quick and easy little gift for someone that you care about. The Painted Stars (see page 13) work especially well for the cards.

Holiday Ornament

The Sweet Dreams, Glimmer, Gratitude, and Clancy Stars make wonderful hanging ornaments for the holidays. See the instructions for the Brooch or Shawl Pin on page 19, the Smiling Star on page 17, Painted Stars on page 13, and Little Gifts on page 26. Stitch smaller crocheted stars, beads, buttons, charms, and found objects to embellish the ornaments.

Use yarn, thread, or ribbon to make the hanging loop and embellish with beads.

Starry Socks

I love knitting socks and enjoy embellishing the cuffs with flowers and other lighthearted fripperies, so I couldn't resist adding Glimmer Stars (Sweet Dreams Stars would work well too) to the cuffs of this pair of ankle socks that I was knitting at the same time as writing this book. Crossover happens! I used a US size C/D (3 mm) hook to crochet five stars for each sock; then I stitched the top points to the edge of the cuff, evenly spaced. They put a sparkle in my step and make me smile. We all need a little whimsy, don't we? If you don't make your own socks, you can still add stars to your store-bought socks to make them uniquely your own. Feel free to add beads as well, just for a little more twinkle!

Acknowledgments

*t*hank you so much to the skillful and pleasant people at Stackpole Books, especially to: Candi Derr, Mary Wheelehan, Tessa Sweigert, Caroline Stover, and Judith Schnell, and thank you also to Lion Brand Yarn for supplying the lovely yarns for this book. I am deeply grateful to my counselor, Dr. William Ramer, and my grief counselor, Theresa Charbonneau, who guided, mentored, supported, and sustained me through the ravages of my journey in grieving the death of my beloved son-in-law, Clancy. I could not have written this book without their compassionate wisdom and presence.